GEOGRAPHY OF THE US NORTHEAST STATES

(NEW YORK, NEW JERSEY, MAINE, MASSACHUSETTS AND MORE)

GEOGRAPHY FOR KIDS
US STATES
5TH GRADE SOCIAL STUDIES

Speedy Publishing LLC

40 E. Main St. #1156

Newark, DE 19711

www.speedypublishing.com

Copyright 2017

In this book, we're going to talk about the geography of the northeast states of the United States. So, let's get right to it!

The northeast states have beautiful coastal areas with sandy beaches, marshland, and offshore islands. They also have river valleys with fertile farmland and areas of dense trees. The picturesque mountain regions are extensions of the Appalachian Mountains and the highest peak in the northeast is in New Hampshire.

APPALACHIAN MOUNTAINS

NEW ENGLAND COASTLINE

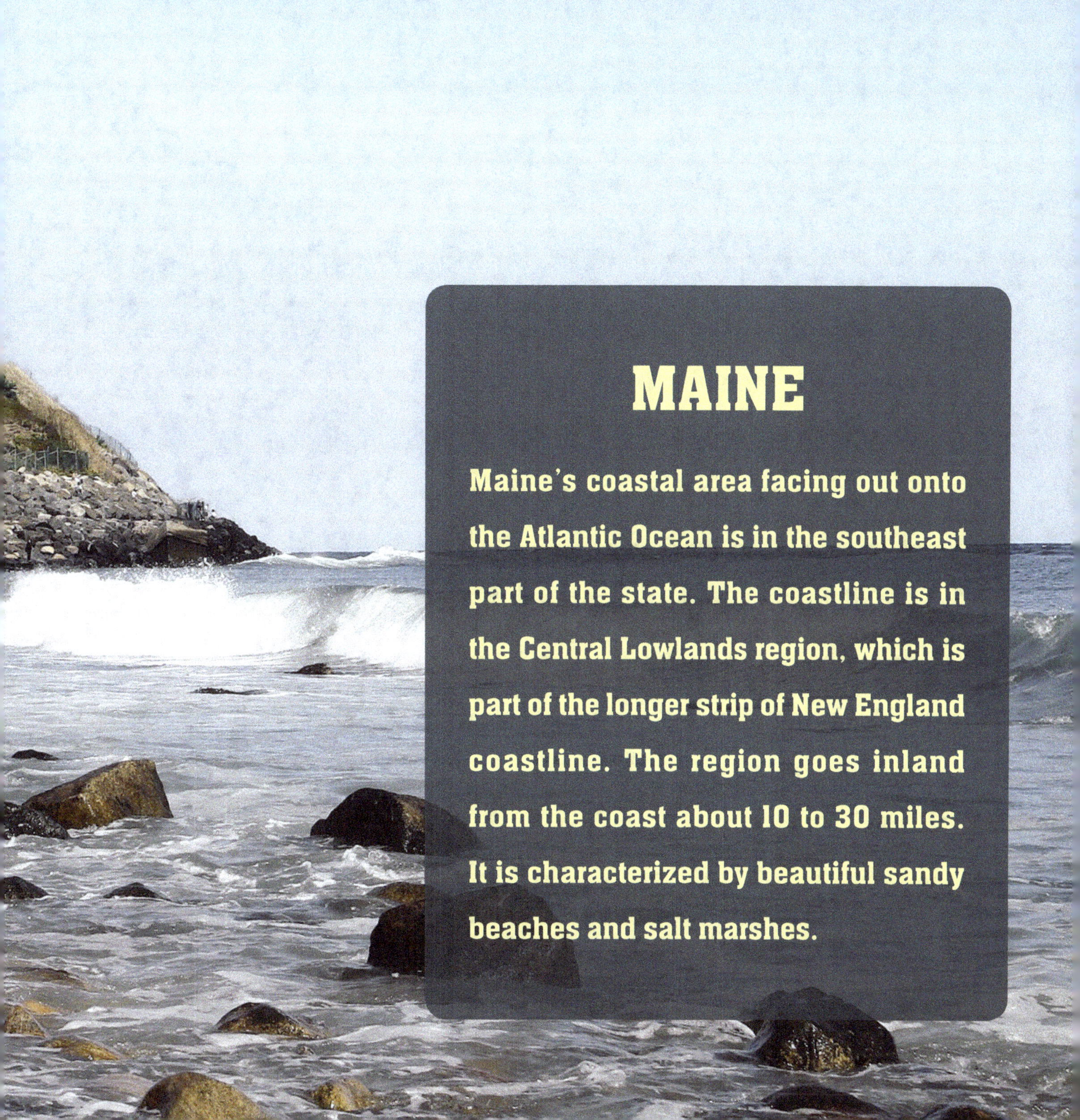

MAINE

Maine's coastal area facing out onto the Atlantic Ocean is in the southeast part of the state. The coastline is in the Central Lowlands region, which is part of the longer strip of New England coastline. The region goes inland from the coast about 10 to 30 miles. It is characterized by beautiful sandy beaches and salt marshes.

There are hundreds of small islands off Maine's coast as well. In the western part of the state, the White Mountains region enters the state from its neighbor Vermont. In Maine, these mountains are described as the Longfellow Range. The highest peaks in the state are located here including Mount Katahdin, which is a height of 5,268 feet.

MOUNT KATAHDIN

AROOSTOOK PLATEAU

Between the Central Lowlands and the White Mountain regions is the Eastern New England Upland region. This region of plateaus is separated by mountain streams and lakes. The Aroostook Plateau is in the northeast section of this region and is well known for its potato crops. Maine has many large natural lakes and the Penobscot and the Kennebec are its most important rivers.

NEW HAMPSHIRE

A piece of the southeastern corner of New Hampshire is in the Coastal Lowlands region. This narrow band of land runs up the New England coast and includes many beaches facing out on the Atlantic Ocean. Most of the southern and western part of the state is covered by the Eastern New England Upland region.

NEW HAMPSHIRE

MANZI DODGE
MERRIMACK RIVER

This region includes the Merrimack River Valley, which is located in the south-central portion of the state. There are many natural lakes located east of this valley at the border with Maine.

Along much of the western border is the valley formed by the Connecticut River, which has fertile soil for farming. The White Mountains region lies between the two river valleys. It is part of the northernmost region of the Appalachian Mountains that extend into western Maine.

Due to its dense forests, New Hampshire has a thriving paper industry. The state's highest peak is Mount Washington, which has a height of 6,288 feet and is the highest peak in all of the northeast states.

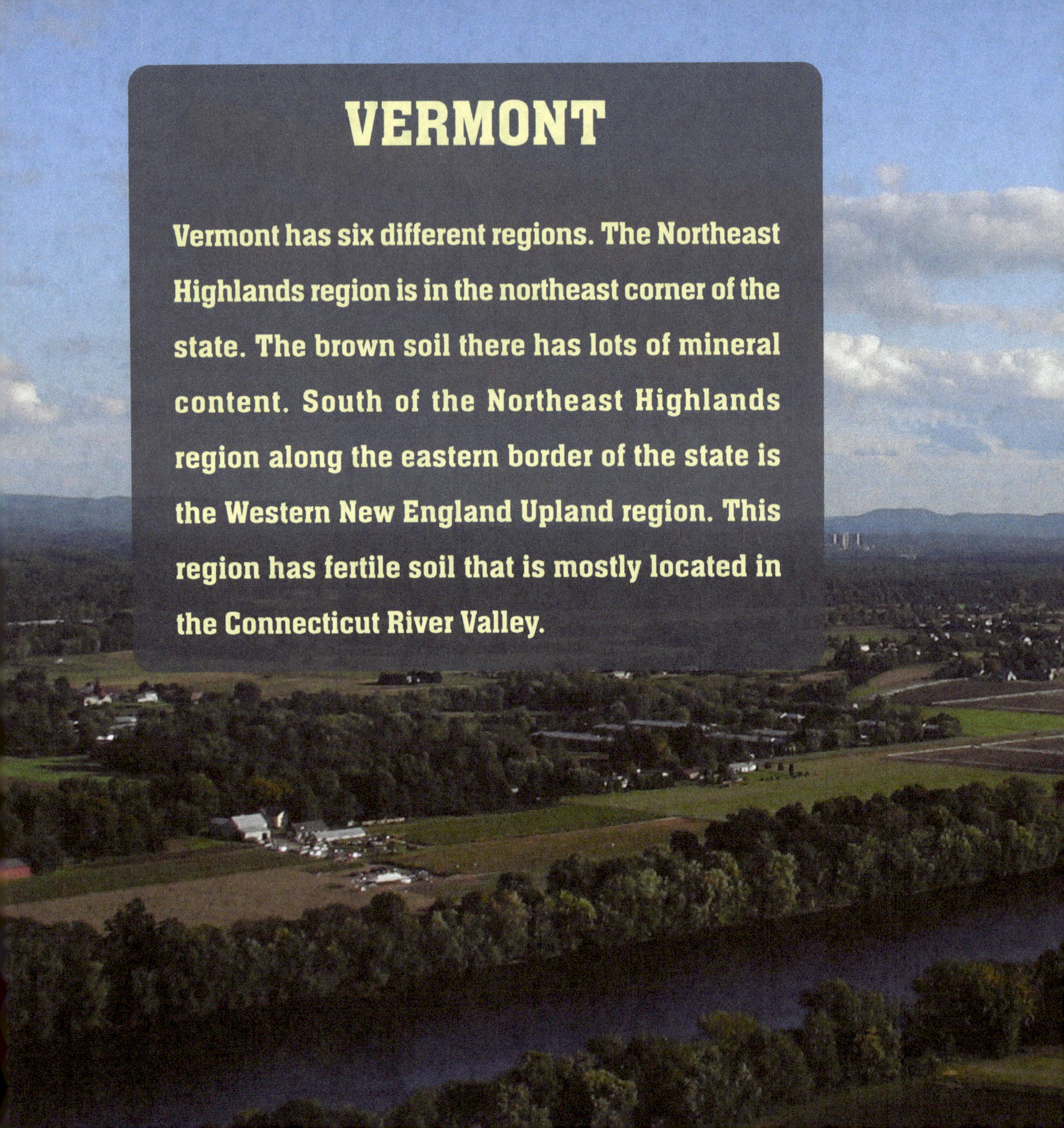

VERMONT

Vermont has six different regions. The Northeast Highlands region is in the northeast corner of the state. The brown soil there has lots of mineral content. South of the Northeast Highlands region along the eastern border of the state is the Western New England Upland region. This region has fertile soil that is mostly located in the Connecticut River Valley.

CONNECTICUT RIVER

MT. MANSFIELD

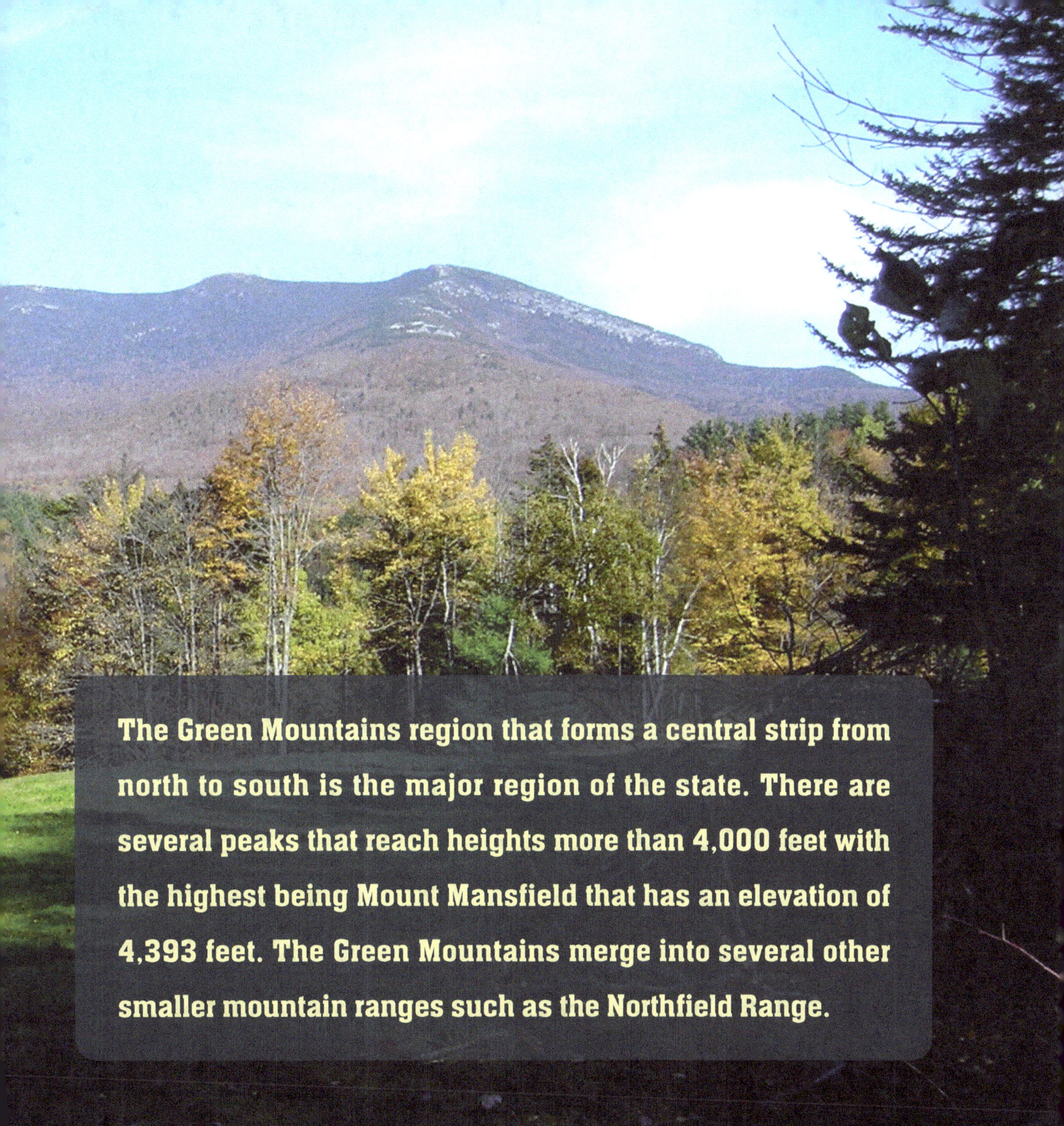

The Green Mountains region that forms a central strip from north to south is the major region of the state. There are several peaks that reach heights more than 4,000 feet with the highest being Mount Mansfield that has an elevation of 4,393 feet. The Green Mountains merge into several other smaller mountain ranges such as the Northfield Range.

West of the Green Mountain region are some low valleys with the Vermont Valley in the southwest. It is a narrow strip of land between the Green Mountains and the Taconic Mountains.

The Taconic Mountains region extends from the state of Massachusetts into Vermont's southwestern section. Along Vermont's western border with the state of New York is the Champlain Valley.

It surrounds Lake Champlain, which is Vermont's largest natural lake and also is the largest natural lake in New England.

CAPE COD

MASSACHUSETTS

The eastern part of Massachusetts is part of the Coastal Lowlands region. It extends about 40 miles inland from the coast. This region includes Cape Cod as well as other islands off the coast. West of the Coastal Lowlands region is the Eastern New England Uplands region, which is an extension of New Hampshire's White Mountains.

The terrain gradually slopes toward the coast in the east and the Connecticut River Valley to the west. The Connecticut Valley Lowland region, which runs from north to south within the state, is a very fertile region that is used for farming.

CONNECTICUT RIVER VALLEY

GREEN MOUNTAINS

The western portion of the state is in the Western New England Upland region. It is primarily composed of the Berkshire Hills, which is an extension of Vermont's Green Mountains. The Taconic Mountains region crosses the northwestern section of the state.

There are more than 4,000 miles of river waterways within the state including the Connecticut River, which is New England's longest river.

CONNECTICUT RIVER

RHODE ISLAND

RHODE ISLAND

Rhode Island only has two distinct regions of terrain. The Coastal Lowlands region covers the eastern portion of the state. It's dominated by Narragansett Bay and the other bays, islands, and inlets. There are rocky shorelines, sandy beaches, and salt marshes. Rhode Island has 36 separate islands off its coast that are part of its land area. The largest is Aquidneck Island, which is 45 miles across. The northwestern portion of the state is in the New England Upland region. The highest elevation, Jerimoth Hill, is located there, but it is only 812 feet high.

CONNECTICUT

The Coastal Lowlands region runs the entire southern width of the state. It is a narrow band of flat rocky ridges and beaches.

The Connecticut Valley Lowlands region, which is formed
by the Connecticut River, separates the state in half running
from north to south.

The eastern portion of the state is the Eastern New England Upland region, which is an area of hills and valleys. Elevations of 1,200 feet are found in the northwest portion of this region and the land slopes down toward the southeast where the elevations are no higher than 500 feet.

Most of the western part of the state is covered by the Western New England Upland region, the southernmost portion of the Berkshire Hills. In the far northwest corner, the Taconic Range is separated from the Berkshire Hills by the Housatonic River. Located there is the highest point in the state, Mount Frissell.

HOUSATONIC RIVER

HUDSON RIVER VALLEY

NEW YORK

New York City and Long Island are at the southeastern end of the state. These highly populated areas are in the Atlantic Coastal Plain region. North of this area is the New England Upland region, which runs north along the Hudson River Valley's eastern bank. The Hudson-Mohawk Lowland region follows the Hudson River Valley's western bank. Then, it makes a turn to the northwest and encompasses the Mohawk River valley.

West of the Mohawk River's headwaters is the Tug Hill Plateau region. The northeastern part of the state lies in the Adirondack Upland region. The highest elevations in the state are found in the Adirondacks with the highest at Mount Marcy, a height of 5,344 feet.

Across the northern border of the state is the St. Lawrence Lowland region. The Appalachian Plateau region runs along a large portion of the southern regions of the state.

CENTRAL CATSKILLS

Much of this region's eastern section is the Catskill Mountains. The Erie-Ontario Lowland region is situated along the northwest border of the state below the St. Lawrence River, which separates New York from Canada, and is east of Lake Erie and Lake Ontario.

NEW JERSEY

New Jersey's southern and eastern sections are in the Atlantic Coastal Plain region. This region is mostly flat and just above sea level. The coastline has lots of popular vacation-destination beaches as well as an abundance of marshes. The eastern portion of this region, called Pine Barrens, consists of sandy soil with short scrub pines. This large area soaks up and transmits groundwater. Inland from the sandy coast is soil that is suitable for farming. The Piedmont Lowlands region is located northwest of the Coastal Plain region.

PINE BARRENS

KITTATINNY MOUNTAIN

North of the Piedmont is the Highlands region, which has steep ridges and lots of natural lakes. The northwestern part of the state is in the Appalachian Valley region, which consists of the Kittatinny Mountains and numerous valleys with fertile soil. The Kittatinny range is part of the Appalachian Mountain range. The highest point of the state is 1,803 feet and is appropriately named High Point.

PENNSYLVANIA

Pennsylvania has several different types of regions. In the southeast corner of the state is a small strip of the Atlantic Coastal Plain region. It runs in a northeast to southwest direction. Further inland and parallel to this region is the Piedmont region, which has gently rolling hills with rich soil perfect for farming. Most of the central and northeastern section of Pennsylvania is dominated by the Appalachian Ridge and Valley region.

SUSQUEHANNA RIVER

This area includes the beautiful Pocono Mountains with the Susquehanna River valley cutting through. Extending north into the state all the way from the state of Georgia is the Blue Ridge region, which crosses the southern border in a narrow piece.

The Appalachian Plateau region takes up the northern and western areas of the state. This rugged landscape has steep valleys and the highest elevations in the state. The highest elevation is Mount Davis, which has a height of 3,213 feet. The Erie Lowland region is a narrow band of land that borders Lake Erie in the northwest corner of the state. The New England Upland region forms a very small ridge of land between the Piedmont and the Appalachian Ridge and Valley regions.

MOUNT DAVIS

The northeast region is primarily part of the Appalachian Highlands region, but large sections are part of the Atlantic Coastal Plain region, which extends south to the tip of Florida.

The coastal plain regions are flat with sandy beaches and marshes. The highlands have rolling hills and dense forests. There are many river valleys with fertile farmlands.

Awesome! Now that you've read about the geography of the northeast section of the United States, you may want to read about the geography of the southern states in the Baby Professor book Geography of the US – South Region States (Texas, Florida, Delaware and More) | Geography for Kids.

Rough Ridge Tunnel

Visit
BABY PROFESSOR
EDUCATION KIDS
www.BabyProfessorBooks.com
to download Free Baby Professor eBooks
and view our catalog of new and exciting
Children's Books